What to Say

words for all occasions

What to Say

words for all occasions

PENGUIN BOOKS

PENGUIN BOOKS

Published by the Penguin Group
Penguin Group (Australia)
250 Camberwell Road, Camberwell, Victoria 3124, Australia
(a division of Pearson Australia Group Pty Ltd)
Penguin Group (USA) Inc.
375 Hudson Street, New York, New York 10014, USA
Penguin Group (Canada)
90 Eglinton Avenue East, Suite 700, Toronto ON M4P 2Y3, Canada
(a division of Pearson Penguin Canada Inc.)
Penguin Books Ltd
80 Strand, London WC2R 0RL, England
Penguin Ireland
25 St Stephen's Green, Dublin 2, Ireland
(a division of Penguin Books Ltd)
Penguin Books India Pvt Ltd
11 Community Centre, Panchsheel Park, New Delhi – 110 017, India
Penguin Group (NZ)
67 Apollo Drive, Rosedale, North Shore 0632, New Zealand
(a division of Pearson New Zealand Ltd)
Penguin Books (South Africa) (Pty) Ltd
24 Sturdee Avenue, Rosebank, Johannesburg 2196, South Africa

Penguin Books Ltd, Registered Offices: 80 Strand, London, WC2R 0RL,
England

First published by Penguin Group (Australia), 2006

10 9 8 7 6 5

Text copyright © Penguin Group (Australia) 2006
Written by Victoria Heywood

The moral right of the author has been asserted

Text and cover design by Elizabeth Theodosiadis © Penguin Group (Australia)
Cover illustration by Lisa Coutts
Typeset in Mrs Eaves by Post Pre-press Group, Maryborough, Victoria
Printed in Australia by Mcpherson's Printing Group, Mulgrave, Victoria

National Library of Australia
Cataloguing-in-Publication data:

What to say
ISBN 978 0 14 300493 6

1. Interpersonal communication. 2. Oral communication.
3. Letter writing. 4. Bad news.

302.224

penguin.com.au

Contents

Introduction

If you sometimes find it difficult to know what to say, you are not alone. Whether it's congratulating someone on their marriage, writing a birthday message for a colleague or offering condolences to the recently bereaved, many of us struggle to find the right words.

We all want what we say to be both meaningful and memorable — for the right reasons, that is. No one wants to be remembered for being the one who made the birthday girl cry or insulted the host. Being able to get your feelings across with wit, thought, care, sympathy or heartfelt honesty will be appreciated by the recipient, and your message will linger in their thoughts long after the event has passed. Something written in a card, or said with love, can become a treasured keepsake or memory.

Of course, some things are best said in person — apologies, for instance, or declarations of love. Others require a more formal written note, a card or perhaps an email.

But while it can be tempting just to stammer out a few platitudes, or to buy a card with an impersonal message and sign your name, nothing beats the personal touch. Even just adding one imaginative sentence to a commercial card will bring so much more meaning to your message. Experiment with classy stationary too — gorgeous paper and a handwritten note or carefully chosen poem will have far more impact.

Think about your target audience. Great Aunt Alice is unlikely to appreciate the kind of jocular birthday greetings you might send your very best friend. You also need to think about what you want to achieve with your message — whether you want the recipient of your words to feel loved, comforted, reprimanded or inspired. And take a deep breath before you open your mouth or set pen to paper. A moment's reflection is worth a lifetime of regret for things said or unsaid.

To help you find the right words, this book includes suggestions for things to say both in person and when writing. For handy reference, it is divided into sections on some of the most common occasions when special words are called for — farewells, weddings, births, deaths, anniversaries, birthdays, thanks, congratulations and many more.

Each section includes ideas that you can adapt to suit the particular recipient or circumstances — these can either be written or spoken. There is also a selection of quotable quotes and relevant poems that may add just the touch you're looking for.

Poems make a good addition to a formal ceremony too, and the ones chosen for this book have resonated down the centuries for a very good reason — they express universal truths, beautifully, simply and with imagination. Let these words inspire you.

Babies,
birthdays
and begetters

Births

The birth of a child is a life-changing occasion for all concerned. The proud new parents are likely to believe that their baby is the best, brightest and most beautiful ever born, so even if the infant in question looks like a jaundiced bulldog, be tactful. And never make comparisons with your own children and experiences — right now, all they want to hear is how clever they are for having produced such a wonder.

Spoken from the heart

Look at all of you!
What a gorgeous family you make!

⌐

You must be feeling so happy and proud.
Congratulations and well done!

⌐

It's a miracle!
I never thought you had it in you!

⌐

I am so pleased for you all. He/she's absolutely
perfect in every way — right down to his/her
father's nose/mum's eyes.

⌐

So this is the one that caused so much trouble!
For everyone's sake, here's hoping he/she sleeps
like a baby now.

⌐

What a gorgeous baby! And look at his/her
beautiful little fingers. I can tell you're
wrapped around them already.

⌐

Welcome to the world, kid. And welcome to
the world of nappies, Mum and Dad.

Written with care

As Dorothy Parker once said, 'I always knew
you had it in you.' Congratulations on the
birth of your son/daughter.

∽

We're delighted to welcome _____ to the
extended family. Congratulations to you both,
and we hope he/she brings you a lifetime of joy.

∽

Here's a little gift to mark the birth of your
baby son/daughter. With all our love and
congratulations on a tough job well done.

∽

Our thoughts are with you on this momentous
occasion. Here's something for your new
family, with all our love.

∽

Having seen how hard you guys can party,
we couldn't think of better candidates for the
night shift! Congratulations!

∽

Welcome to the parenthood club. Now it's
time to wave goodbye to the months
of anticipation and say hello to the months
of sleep deprivation.

～

They say that life will never be the same again.
They're right. With gorgeous _____ in
your family, it'll get better every day.

～

May _____ fill your home with laughter,
love, joy and friends. Congratulations on the
new addition to the family.

Quotable quotes

Every baby born into the world is a finer
one than the last.

Nicholas Nickleby, CHARLES DICKENS

～

Infancy conforms to nobody; all conform to it.

RALPH WALDO EMERSON

～

So for the mother's sake the child was dear,

And dearer was the mother for the child.

SAMUEL TAYLOR COLERIDGE

⌒

A baby is an angel whose wings decrease as
his legs increase.

FRENCH PROVERB

⌒

A baby is an inestimable blessing and bother.

MARK TWAIN

⌒

Heaven is at the feet of Mothers.

ARABIC PROVERB

In others' words

A Baby's feet, like sea-shells pink,

Might tempt, should heaven see meet,

An angel's lips to kiss, we think,

A baby's feet.

Etude Realiste, ALGERNON CHARLES SWINBURNE

⌒

No rosebuds yet by dawn impearled
Match, even in loveliest lands,
The sweetest flowers in all the world —
A baby's hands.

Etude Realiste, ALGERNON CHARLES SWINBURNE

A baby shines as bright
If winter or if May be
On eyes that keep in sight
A baby.
Though dark the skies or grey be,
It fills our eyes with light,
If midnight or midday be.
Love hails it, day and night,
The sweetest thing that may be
Yet cannot praise aright
A baby.

Babyhood, ALGERNON CHARLES SWINBURNE

Soul's Birth

When you were born, beloved, was your soul
New made by God to match your body's flower,
And were they both at one same precious hour
Sent forth from heaven as a perfect whole?
Or had your soul since dim creation burned,
A star in some still region of the sky,
That leaping earthward, left its place on high
And to your little new-born body yearned?
No words can tell in what celestial hour
God made your soul and gave it mortal birth,
Nor in the disarray of all the stars
Is any place so sweet that such a flower
Might linger there until thro' heaven's bars,
It heard God's voice that bade it down to earth.

SARA TEASDALE

⁓

The Angel that presided o'er my birth
Said, 'Little creature, form'd of Joy and Mirth,
Go love without the help of any Thing
on Earth.'

WILLIAM BLAKE

⁓

Lullaby of the Iroquois

Little brown baby-bird, lapped in your nest,
Wrapped in your nest,
Strapped in your nest,
Your straight little cradle-board rocks
you to rest;
Its hands are your nest;
Its bands are your nest;
It swings from the down-bending branch
of the oak;
You watch the camp flame, and the curling
grey smoke;
But, oh, for your pretty black eyes sleep
is best,—
Little brown baby of mine, go to rest.
Little brown baby-bird swinging to sleep,
Winging to sleep,
Singing to sleep,
Your wonder-black eyes that so wide
open keep,
Shielding their sleep,
Unyielding to sleep,

The heron is homing, the plover is still,
The night-owl calls from his haunt on the hill,
Afar the fox barks, afar the stars peep,—
Little brown baby of mine, go to sleep.

EMILY PAULINE JOHNSON (TEKAHIONWAKE)

Birthdays

A birthday is a personal occasion
and your message likewise should be
tailored to the recipient. Only you will
know how far you can go with humour.
If your friend is sensitive about their age,
perhaps it would be more tactful to focus
on the wonderful times you have shared
over the years than on their receding
hairline. For someone with a more robust
sense of humour, feel free to poke fun.
Or choose an appropriate quote from the
ones outlined below, perhaps written
on a handmade card and accompanied
with a brief, personal message.

Spoken from the heart

Happy birthday. You really do deserve
everything you get today!

*(Suitable for friends or even someone you don't
particularly like!)*

⌒

Have a great day. I hope all your birthday
wishes come true.

⌒

Oooh, look at you. You don't look a day
older than you did yesterday!

⌒

Happy birthday _____, and thanks
for being such a special part of my life.

⌒

Have a fantastic birthday, kiddo. I look forward
to celebrating many more of them with you.

⌒

I do hope you're not worried about getting
another year older. Think of it as another year
to eat chocolate/go shopping/play golf.

⌒

You look different somehow. What's changed?
I know! You're another year older!

Written with care

Don't worry about getting older. It's better
than the alternative.

⌣

Now that you're old enough to know better,
you're old enough to *really* misbehave!

⌣

Happy birthday sweetheart. I knew you'd love
a delicious meal that you didn't have to prepare
yourself . . . so here's the local takeaway menu.

⌣

Happy ___ th birthday, old timer.
(So what *was* it like in the olden days?)

⌣

With lots of love on your very special day.
Hope it's packed full of pleasant surprises.

⌣

Don't worry about getting older . . . just enjoy
the cake while you still have all your own teeth.

⌣

You're not 40! You're 21 with 19 years
of experience!

⤳

On your birthday, I just wanted you to
know that you get better every year.

⤳

Happy birthday, and thanks for so many
years of happy memories.

⤳

You happened to mention that it's your
___ th birthday today. (But what does your
birth certificate say?!)

⤳

May your birthday celebrations go off with
a bang. I feel so privileged to be able to
share them with you.

⤳

On your birthday, I look back on all the good
and bad times we've laughed and cried our way
through. Thank you for being there with me.

⤳

Don't worry, my friend. You're not
really getting older — just more like your
mother/father!

～

Take care of your appearance and try to behave
yourself. Remember, you don't have as long
now to live down those embarrassing moments.

～

You're not another year older — just a day
older than you were yesterday.

～

On your birthday, I'd just like to thank you
for being someone who makes a difference.

～

Congratulations on reaching the grand
old age of ___. May there be many more
birthdays to come.

～

Welcome to your third/fourth/fifth decade!

Quotable quotes

There are 364 days when you might get
unbirthday presents . . . and only one
for birthday presents, you know.

Through the Looking Glass, LEWIS CARROLL

❧

Youth, large, lusty, loving — Youth, full
of grace, force, fascination.

Do you know that Old Age may come after
you with equal grace, force, fascination?

WALT WHITMAN

❧

Your lordship, though not clean past your
youth, hath yet some smack of age in you,
some relish of the saltness of time.

King Henry IV, WILLIAM SHAKESPEARE

❧

At twenty years of age, the will reigns; at thirty,
the wit; and at forty, the judgement.

HENRY GRATTAN

❧

May you live all the days of your life.

JONATHAN SWIFT

❧

What's a man's age? He must hurry more,
that's all;
Cram in a day what his youth took
a year to hold.

ROBERT BROWNING

⌒

If youth, but knew, if old age but could.

HENRI ESTIENNE

⌒

An old man loved is winter with flowers.

GERMAN PROVERB

In others' words

To pass our youth in dull indifference,
to refuse the sweets of life because they once
must leave us, is as preposterous as to wish
to have been born old because we one day must
be old. For my part, my youth may wear and
waste, but it shall never rust in my possession.

WILLIAM CONGREVE

⌒

Alas, that Spring should vanish with the Rose!

That Youth's sweet-scented Manuscript
should close!

The Nightingale that in the Branches sang,

Ah, whence, and whither flown again,
who knows!

The Rubáiyát of Omar Khayyám,
EDWARD MARLBOROUGH FITZGERALD

∽

To keep the heart unwrinkled, to be hopeful,
kindly, cheerful, reverent — that is to triumph
over old age.

Leaves from a Notebook in Ponkapog Papers,
THOMAS BAILEY ALDRICH

∽

Gather ye rosebuds while ye may,

Old Time is still a-flying;

And this same flower that smiles today

Tomorrow will be dying.

To the Virgins, to Make Much of Time,
ROBERT HERRICK

Mothers and Fathers Day

Think about all your mother and father
have done for you over the years . . .
you know they deserve more than a
shop-bought card with a hastily
scrawled signature.

Spoken from the heart

I don't tell you nearly often enough how much you mean to me. Lucky there's this one day a year.

⌒

Thank you for putting up with me for all these years! I know there have been times when you could have happily swapped me.

⌒

Today's your day, so I want you to take it easy and relax. Just something simple for dinner will be fine!

⌒

I love you Mum/Dad. And I promise that I'll tell you that more often.

⌒

I know it goes against the natural order of things, but just for today, I'm going to do everything you want me to . . .

⌒

You know I'm not very good at putting my feelings into words, Mum/Dad. So I hope my actions show you how much you mean to me.

Written with care

I just wanted to say how lucky I am to have a
Mum/Dad who's so patient, kind, funny . . .
and rich!

⌒

To the best cook/cleaner/driver/chief bottle
washer in the family business.

⌒

To Mum/Dad. You gave me everything that
made me the person I am today — well, half
of it, anyway.

⌒

To my one and only Mum/Dad. Thanks
for everything you have ever given me, but
thank you most of all for your love.

⌒

Thanks for always being there for me — I
appreciate all that you are and all that you do.

⌒

Mum/Dad we love you! We're so lucky to
have you in our lives. Thank you.

⌒

You're the kind of parent who makes
me want to be the best I can be.

❧

To the best and fairest Mum/Dad in the world.
Happy Mothers/Fathers Day!

Quotable quotes

Children suck the mother when they are
young and the father when they are old.

ENGLISH PROVERB

❧

One father is more than a hundred
schoolmasters.

GEORGE HERBERT

❧

We think our fathers fools, so wise we grow;
Our wiser sons, no doubt will think us so.

ALEXANDER POPE

❧

The mother's heart is the child's schoolroom.

HENRY WARD BEECHER

❧

Any man can be a father, but it takes
a special person to be a dad.

ANON.

⌐

A father is someone who carries pictures
where his money used to be.

ANON.

⌐

The happy family is but an earlier heaven.

SIR JOHN BOWRING

⌐

Men are what their mothers made them.

RALPH WALDO EMERSON

⌐

Mother is the name for God in the lips
and hearts of little children.

WILLIAM MAKEPEACE THACKERAY

⌐

God could not be everywhere and
therefore he made mothers.

JEWISH PROVERB

⌐

It is not flesh and blood, but heart which
makes us fathers and sons.

JOHANN FRIEDRICH VON SCHILLER

In others' words

When I was a boy of fourteen, my father was so
ignorant I could hardly stand to have the old
man around. But when I got to be twenty-one,
I was astonished at how much he had learned
in seven years.

MARK TWAIN

For all of us, kisses seemed to spring from
her eyes, which could not look upon those
she loved without seeming to bestow upon
them passionate caresses.

Remembrance of Things Past, MARCEL PROUST

A mighty power and stronger
Man from his throne has hurled,
For the hand that rocks the cradle
Is the hand that rules the world.

WILLIAM ROSS WALLACE

Amity
and amour

Friendship

Your true friends are those who are there beside you through the good times and the bad. You trust them with your secrets, your hopes and your fears — but how often do you tell them how much they mean to you? Saying a few words to express your appreciation can go a long way.

Spoken from the heart

I know I don't say it often enough, but
I hope you realise how much your friendship
means to me.

⌒

The nicest thing about having a friend like
you is that I know I can count on you to be
there for me, whatever happens. Thanks.

⌒

You're a true friend — honest, loyal and
always prepared to lend me a fiver/babysit/give
me an alibi when I need it!

⌒

Thanks for listening to me bang on about
_____. You're always so patient and give
great advice. You really are a true friend.

Written with care

True friends never quit. Thanks for sticking
by me during a rough patch.

⌒

Thanks for being the kind of friend who's not afraid to tell me a few home truths. Your honesty is important to me.

⁓

Just a quick note to let you know how much I value your friendship. Your phone number will always remain top of my speed-dial list.

⁓

To the most giving, considerate and loving person I know. Thanks for being such a good friend.

⁓

To my favourite champagne drinking/gossip/ shopping partner, thanks for being there when it counts.

⁓

Here's to the ups and downs of friendship – and to lots more of the ups and lots less of the downs!

⁓

Thanks for bringing a smile to my face for the first time in ages. I couldn't have made it without you.

⁓

To my very bestest friend. Thanks for being
beside me through thick and thin, sick and sin.

Quotable quotes

A friend is a person with whom I may be
sincere. Before him I may think aloud.

RALPH WALDO EMERSON

~

There is no better looking glass than
an old friend.

ENGLISH PROVERB

~

The road to a friend's house is never long.

DANISH PROVERB

~

True friends stab you in the front.

OSCAR WILDE

~

A friend is one who knows you and loves
you just the same.

ELBERT GREEN HUBBARD

~

Friendship is like a prism through which
the many variations of beauty are revealed
in our lives.

ANON.

⤴

Friendship, the wine of life, should, like a well-
stocked cellar, be thus continually renewed.

SAMUEL JOHNSON

⤴

The firmest friendships have been formed
in mutual adversity, as iron is most strongly
united by the fiercest flame.

CHARLES CALEB COLTON

⤴

A faithful friend is the medicine of life.

The Bible, ECCLESIASTES 6:16

⤴

In prosperity our friends know us;
In adversity we know our friends.

JOHN CHURTON COLLINS

In others' words

What is so great as friendship, let us carry
with what grandeur of spirit we can. Let us
be silent, — so we may hear the whisper of the
gods. Let us not interfere. Who set you to cast
about what you should say to the select souls,
or how to say any thing to such? No matter
how ingenious, no matter how graceful and
bland. There are innumerable degrees of folly
and wisdom, and for you to say aught is to be
frivolous. Wait, and thy heart shall speak. Wait
until the necessary and everlasting overpowers
you, until day and night avail themselves of
your lips. The only reward of virtue is virtue;
the only way to have a friend is to be one.

RALPH WALDO EMERSON

Be courteous to all, but intimate with few, and
let those few be well tried before you give them
your confidence. True friendship is a plant of
slow growth, and must undergo and withstand
the shocks of adversity before it is entitled to
the appellation.

GEORGE WASHINGTON

But Oh! The blessing it is to have a friend to whom one can speak fearless on any subject; with whom one's deepest as well as one's most foolish thoughts come out simply and safely. Oh, the comfort — *the inexpressible comfort of feeling safe with a person* — having neither to weigh thoughts nor measure words, but pouring them all right out, just as they are, chaff and grain together; certain that a faithful hand will take and sift them, keep what is worth keeping, and then with the breath of kindness blow the rest away.

A Life for a Life,
DINAH MARIA MULOCK CRAIK

In poverty and other misfortunes of life, true friends are a sure refuge. The young they keep out of mischief; to the old they are a comfort and aid in their weakness, and those in the prime of life they incite to noble deeds.

ARISTOTLE

Love

Confessing your feelings of love can be
both exquisitely joyous and excruciatingly
painful. Just remember that people tend
to keep and treasure anything written,
so never post a letter or hit send on an
email until you've re-read your words and
are completely happy with the message
they convey. Remember too, that the best
words of love are simple, spontaneous
and sincere. They should reflect your time
together, your hopes for the future and
your feelings for your loved one.

Spoken from the heart

Words can't describe what I feel. So I hope my actions show you exactly how much I love you.

⌐

You may be just one person in the world. But you are my entire world. I love you.

⌐

Thank you for being you and being mine.

⌐

I want you to know that there is absolutely nothing I would not do for you. But you may have to ask me a couple of times.

⌐

I am so happy you are here in my life, walking alongside me into the future.

⌐

Let me hold you forever.

⌐

As a wife/husband, lover, friend and companion, you are the very best. You're also not bad at golf/cards/cooking/fixing things.

⌐

Until I met you, I didn't know what true love was. Now I've experienced love in your arms, I'll never want for anything or anyone else.

Written with care

When I wake in the morning, the echo of your laughter is the first thing that I hear. When I go to sleep at night, I close my eyes and see your face. I dream of you during the night's dark hours. And during the long days I think only of when we will meet again.

When I'm with you, I feel more intensely alive, more aware of wonder, more intensely myself than ever before. Breathing, hearing, touching, tasting, seeing — you are the first one to awaken all my senses. Nobody has brought the world to life for me in this way before. You amaze me.

I don't have much time, but I just wanted to say that when you walked away from me today, part of me went with you. Take care of my heart until you return.

I've been sitting here for half an hour, trying
to think of what to say to you about last night.
There are so many great sweeping ideas
I've written and discarded. Because in the end,
it comes down to three simple words.
I love you.

⌒

Think of me when you hear music.
Think of me when you see sunlight reflected
in a raindrop. Think of me, and know that
I'm yours.

⌒

People keep asking me what I'm smiling about.
Only you know the reason why.

⌒

Thank you for sharing all of yourself with me.

⌒

Trust is a funny thing. We've both been
through so much that, understandably, we were
both wary. But love is a funny thing too. Since
falling in love with you, I've come to trust you
with all my heart.

⌒

Ten things I love about you:

1. Your smile.
2. The way you whistle/hum/kiss.
3. The sound of you singing/laughing.
4. Your enthusiasm for bocce/work.
5. Your passion for poetry/life/sex.
6. How you look when you play with the children/smile at me.
7. Hearing you say 'I love you'/'We'll be together always'.
8. The way you laugh/snore/cook.
9. Your lips/eyes/body.
10. Your love for me and how you show it.

Quotable quotes

Love seeks not to possess, but to be possessed.

ROBERT HUGH BENSON

Who so loves believes the impossible.

ELIZABETH BARRETT BROWNING

Where both deliberate, the love is slight;
Who ever lov'd, that lov'd not at first sight?

CHRISTOPHER MARLOWE

To be beloved is above all bargains.

SEVENTEENTH CENTURY ENGLISH PROVERB

Thou source of all my bliss and all my woe,
That found'st me poor at first, and
keep'st me so.

OLIVER GOLDSMITH

It is impossible to love and be wise.

FRANCIS BACON

Stay me with flagons, comfort me with apples:
for I am sick of love.

The Bible, SONG OF SOLOMON 2:5

Love conquers all: let us too give in to love.

VIRGIL

Love consists in this, that two solitudes
protect and touch and greet each other.

RAINER MARIA RILKE

~

There is no remedy for love but to love more.

HENRY DAVID THOREAU

~

To love and be loved is the greatest
happiness of existence.

SYDNEY SMITH

In others' words

The Passionate Shepherd to His Love

Come live with me, and be my love,
And we will all the pleasures prove,
That valleys, groves, hill and fields,
Woods or steepy mountains yield.

CHRISTOPHER MARLOWE

~

How Do I Love Thee?

How do I love thee? Let me count the ways.
I love thee to the depth and breadth and height
My soul can reach, when feeling out of sight
For the ends of Being and ideal Grace,
I love thee to the level of every day's
Most quiet need, by sun and candle-light.
I love thee freely, as men strive for Right;
I love thee purely, as they turn from Praise.
I love thee with the passion put to use
In my old griefs, and with my childhood's faith:
I love thee with a love I seemed to lose
With my lost saints, — I love thee with
the breath,

Smiles, tears, of all my life! — and,
if God choose,
I shall but love thee better after death.

ELIZABETH BARRETT BROWNING

A Birthday

My heart is like a singing bird
Whose nest is in a watered shoot;
My heart is like an apple tree
Whose boughs are bent with thick-set fruit;
My heart is like a rainbow shell
That paddles in a halcyon sea;
My heart is gladder than all these
Because my love is come to me.
Raise me on a dais of silk and down;
Hang it with vair and purple dyes;
Carve it in doves and pomegranates,
And peacocks with a hundred eyes;
Work it in gold and silver grapes,
In leaves and silver fleurs-de-lys;
Because the birthday of my life
Is come, my love is come to me.

CHRISTINA ROSETTI

My bounty is as boundless as the sea,
My love as deep; the more I give to thee,
The more I have, for both are infinite.

Romeo and Juliet, WILLIAM SHAKESPEARE

⁓

I Would Live In Your Love

I would live in your love as the sea-grasses
live in the sea,

Borne up by each wave as it passes, drawn
down by each wave that recedes;

I would empty my soul of the dreams
that have gathered in me,

I would beat with your heart as it beats,
I would follow your soul as it leads.

SARA TEASDALE

Weddings, parties and anniversaries

Engagements

A couple's public declaration of their
intent to wed is a very special occasion
(even if they have been living together
for ten years, fought like cat and dog
for five and have three kids already).
So whether you think they're mad to
contemplate such a step, or that they're
heading for a marriage made in heaven,
congratulations are in order. The focus of
your message – spoken or written – should
be on their future together.

Spoken from the heart

How happy you both look. You've clearly made
a great decision.

⌒

Congratulations on your exciting news.
Here's to a lifetime of happiness — together!

⌒

We love you, we're proud of the decision you've
made, and we'd be so happy to help out with
arrangements for the wedding in any way.

⌒

About time too.

⌒

Watching you two together has always made
me realise that true love *is* possible.

⌒

I love the way you two look at each other
when you think no-one else is watching.
You're going to make a great team.

⌒

I guess this means there's no hope for me then.

～

You must be so excited. Congratulations
on taking the plunge.

Written with care

Best wishes to you both as you set out
on the next stage of your life together.

～

Congratulations on such great news. Looking
forward to seeing you all frocked up!

～

Best wishes and may your time
together seem timeless.

～

I wish you both a future that's filled
with happiness, laughter and love.

～

All my love, as always, as you set out
on this exciting journey together.

～

Here's hoping all your shared dreams
become reality.

⌒

With lots of love and heartfelt congratulations
to both of you.

⌒

Congratulations on your engagement.
This is a magical time in your life together.
Enjoy every minute of it.

⌒

Here's to love, lifelong companionship
and surviving the wedding. Congratulations
on your engagement, you two.

Quotable quotes

It is a truth universally acknowledged that a
single man in possession of a good fortune
must be in want of a wife.

JANE AUSTEN

⌒

For this cause shall a man leave his father
and mother, and shall be joined unto his wife,
and they two shall be one flesh.

The Bible, EPHESIANS 5:31

～

Keep your eyes wide open before marriage,
half-shut afterwards.

BENJAMIN FRANKLIN

～

Love, *n*: a temporary insanity curable
by marriage or the removal of the
patient from the influences under which
he incurred the disease.

The Devil's Dictionary, AMBROSE BIERCE

～

Courtship to marriage is as a very
witty prologue to a very dull play.

WILLIAM CONGREVE

～

Let men tremble to win the hand of woman,
unless they win along with it the utmost
passion of her heart!

NATHANIEL HAWTHORNE

In others' words

Love is Enough

Love is enough: though the World be a-waning,

And the woods have no voice but the voice
of complaining,

Though the sky be too dark for dim
eyes to discover

The gold-cups and daisies fair blooming
thereunder,

Though the hills be held shadows, and
the sea a dark wonder,

And this day drew a veil o'er all deeds
pass'd over,

Yet their hands shall not tremble, their
feet shall not falter,

The void shall not weary, the fear shall not alter

These lips and these eyes of the loved
and the lover.

WILLIAM MORRIS

Love has no other desire but to fulfil itself.

But if you love and must needs have desires,
let these be desires:

To melt and be like the running brook
that sings its melody to the night.

To know the pain of too much tenderness.

To be wounded by your own understanding
of love;

And to bleed willingly and joyfully.

To wake at dawn with a winged heart and
give thanks for another day of loving;

To rest at the noon hour and meditate
love's ecstasy;

To return home at eventide with gratitude;

And then to sleep with a prayer for
the beloved in

Your heart and a song of praise upon
your lips . . .

The Prophet, KAHLIL GIBRAN

These I Can Promise

I cannot promise you a life of sunshine;
I cannot promise riches, wealth or gold;
I cannot promise you an easy pathway
That leads away from change or growing old.
But I can promise all my heart's devotion
A smile to chase away your tears of sorrow;
A love that's ever true and ever growing;
A hand to hold in yours through each
tomorrow.

MARK TWAIN

Weddings

When you're congratulating the bride and groom on their wedding day, don't just say 'Congratulations!' and scurry off to the bar. Add something personal about your wishes for their life together or make a comment about the ceremony itself, so they know how much you appreciate being part of their special day. Likewise, when writing a card, use words that reflect their personalities, and your own relationship with them. If you don't know one of them particularly well, it can be a nice touch to say how much you look forward to getting to know them or welcoming them into your family. Wedding cards may be kept for a lifetime, so write something that they'll want to read again and again.

Spoken from the heart

Well, you've done it now! Congratulations and here's hoping that the rest of your days together are as happy as this one has been.

 ⌒

It's wonderful to see you both looking so filled with love and joy today.

 ⌒

A word of advice from one who's been here before — whenever things get tough, just remember the love you felt for each other on this day, and the promises you made.

 ⌒

Congratulations. We can tell just by looking at you today that you're both glowing with love from the inside out.

 ⌒

How wonderful to see you exchange your vows, surrounded by all the people who love you most. Thanks for letting me be here with you.

 ⌒

Well done, you two, and we wish you all the happiness that life can bring your way.

⤳

It was such a beautiful ceremony — the music/vows/flowers/setting was magnificent.

⤳

Thanks for inviting us to share in such a special occasion. We are privileged to be here.

⤳

Who would have guessed that both of you would scrub up so well? It all goes to show the transforming power of true love.

Written with care

Congratulations on your wedding. Just remember that the toughest year of marriage is always the one you're in.

⤳

May your happiness be doubled and your sorrows halved. You two make a great couple.

⤳

Hidden inside this card are a million best
wishes for a happy, loving and prosperous
future together as man and wife.

⌐

Wishing you both a lifetime of belly laughs,
back rubs and breakfasts in bed.

⌐

May you both always remain as excited and
happy to see each other as you are today
on your wedding day.

⌐

To a very special couple on their wedding day.
We wish you all the very best for your new
life together.

⌐

Congratulations on choosing someone
you can't live without — not just someone
you can live with!

⌐

As the years pass, may your happiness grow
ever deeper. Best wishes for the future.

⌐

To both of you we wish good luck,
good food and good times together!

~

To a special couple on their special day.
May your future be rich in love, happiness
and dreams that come true.

Quotable quotes

There is no more lovely, friendly and
charming relationship, communion or
company than a good marriage.

MARTIN LUTHER

~

In all of the wedding cake, hope is the
sweetest of plums.

DOUGLAS WILLIAM JERROLD

~

Married couples who love each other tell each
other a thousand things without talking.

CHINESE PROVERB

~

One should believe in marriage as in
the sanctity of the soul.

⌒

True it is that marriages be done in
Heaven and performed on Earth.

William Painter

⌒

Marriage is the perfection of what love
aimed at, ignorant of what it sought.

Ralph Waldo Emerson

In others' words

No love, to love of man and wife;
No hope, to hope of constant heart;
No joy, to joy in wedded life;
No faith, to faith in either part;
Flesh is of flesh, and bone of bone
When deeds and thoughts and words are one.
Thy friend an other friend may be,
But other self is not the same:
Thy spouse the self-same is with thee,

In body, mind, in goods and name:
No thine, no mine, may other call,
Now all is one and one is all.

RICHARD EEDES

~

Now You Will Feel No Rain

Now you will feel no rain,
for each of you will be a shelter to the other.
Now you will feel no cold,
for each of you will be a warmth to the other.
Now there is no loneliness for you,
now there is no more loneliness.
Now you are two bodies,
but there is only one life before you.
Go now to your dwelling place,
to enter into your days together.
And may your days be good
and long on the earth.

TRADITIONAL APACHE PRAYER

~

Though I speak with the tongues of men and
of angels, and have not love, I am become as
sounding brass, or a tinkling cymbal. And
though I have the gift of prophecy, and
understand all mysteries, and all knowledge;
and though I have all faith, so that I could
remove mountains, and I have not love,
I am nothing.

And though I bestow all my goods to feed the
poor, and though I give my body to be burned,
and have not love, it profiteth me nothing.
Love suffereth, and is kind; love envieth not;
love vaunteth not itself, is not puffed up, doth
not behave itself unseemly, seeketh not her
own, is not easily provoked, thinketh no evil,
rejoiceth not in iniquity, but rejoiceth in truth;
beareth all things, believeth all things, hopeth
all things, endureth all things.

Love never faileth, but whether there be
prophecies, they shall fail; whether there be
tongues, they shall cease; whether there be
knowledge, it shall vanish away. For we know in
part, and we prophesy in part. But when that
which is perfect is to come, then that which is
in part shall be done away.

When I was a child, I spake as a child,
I understood as a child, I thought as a child:
but when I became a man, I put away childish
things. For now we see through a glass darkly;
but then face to face. Now I know in part; but
then shall I know even as also I am known. And
now abideth faith, hope, love, these three; but
the greatest of these is love.

The Bible, 1 CORINTHIANS 13

∽

A Marriage

A marriage . . . makes of two fractional lives a
whole; it gives to two purposeless lives a work,
and doubles the strength of each to perform it;
it gives to two questioning natures a reason for
living, and something to live for; it will give a
new gladness to the sunshine, a new fragrance
to the flowers, a new beauty to the earth, and
a new mystery to life.

MARK TWAIN

∽

No Cause or Just Impediment

Let me not to the marriage of true minds
Admit impediments; love is not love
Which alters when it alteration finds,
Or bends with the remover to remove.
O, no, it is an ever-fixed mark
That looks on tempests and is never shaken;
It is the star to every wand'ring bark,
Whose worth's unknown, although his
height be taken.
Love's not Time's fool, though rosy lips
and cheeks
Within his bending sickle's compass come;
Love alters not with his brief hours and weeks,
But bears it out even to the edge of doom.
If this be error and upon me proved,
I never writ, nor no man ever loved.

Sonnet 116, WILLIAM SHAKESPEARE

Anniversaries

On your own anniversary, take a little
time to choose some special words
for the special person in your life. If
congratulating someone else on their
anniversary, keep the message short
and simple, and perhaps focus on what
their partnership may have taught you.
A heartfelt poem or quote can sum this
up beautifully and several examples
are provided here for silver and golden
anniversary celebrations.

Spoken from the heart

Meeting you, falling in love and getting
married is the best thing I have ever done.

❧

Happy anniversary, darling. You may not
be perfect but you're perfect for me.

❧

We've been together for ＿ years now and with
every one that passes, I'm more certain that we
belong together always. Happy anniversary.

❧

I could say a million things to you on this day,
but the four most important words will always
be 'I still love you'.

❧

Our ＿ th anniversary is a reminder
of just how lucky I am.

❧

Happy anniversary! The love that you two
display after all these years is an inspiration
to us all.

❧

You both look just as happy now as you do
in your wedding photos. Congratulations
on your anniversary.

∽

Congratulations on finding the secret
to a successful marriage.

∽

Well, you've made it to number ___. Here's to
lots more happy and fun-filled years together.
You both deserve the very best.

Written with care

To my dearest husband/wife, on the anniversary
of our love affair.

∽

Here's a little something for you on our
anniversary, which I forgot once and never
will again.

∽

You are the person I chose to spend my life
with, and I love you more every day.

∽

On this anniversary of our marriage, I just wanted to say that I love you even more today than on our wedding day. (There's more of you to love, of course).

⤴

Here's to the past we've shared and the future we'll face together. Happy anniversary!

⤴

Happy anniversary! A grand total of ___ years together . . . but who's counting?

⤴

To my dearest husband/wife, you're not just someone I can live with — you're the person I can't live without.

Quotable quotes

Love seems the swiftest, but it is the slowest of growths. No man or woman really knows what perfect love is until they have been married a quarter of a century.

MARK TWAIN

⤴

With fifty years between you and your well-kept
wedding vow, the Golden Age, old friends of
mine, is not a fable now.

JOHN GREENLEAF WHITTIER

❧

Happiness in marriage is entirely a matter
of chance.

Pride and Prejudice, JANE AUSTEN

❧

The fate of a marriage depends on the
first night.

HONORÉ DE BALZAC

In others' words

The Anniversary

Only our love hath no decay;
This, no tomorrow hath, nor yesterday,
Running it never runs from us away,
But truly keeps his first, last, everlasting day.

JOHN DONNE

❧

Marriage hath in it less of beauty but more of
safety than the single life; it hath more care,
but less danger; it is more merry, and more
sad; it is fuller of sorrows, and fuller of joys;
it lies under more burdens, but is supported
by all the strengths of love and charity, and
these burdens are delightful.

JEREMY TAYLOR

⤳

Marriage is one long conversation, chequered
by disputes. Two persons more and more adapt
their notions to suit the other, and
in the process of time, without the sound
of trumpets, they conduct each other into
new worlds of thought.

ROBERT LOUIS STEVENSON

⤳

Sensual pleasure passes and vanishes in the
twinkling of an eye, but the friendship between
us, the mutual confidence, the delights of the
heart, the enchantment of the soul, these things
do not perish and can never be destroyed.

I shall love you until I die.

VOLTAIRE

⤳

To My Dear and Loving Husband

If ever two were one, then surely we.
If ever man were loved by wife, then thee;
If ever wife was happy in a man,
Compare with me ye women if you can.
I prize thy love more than whole mines of gold,
Or all the riches that the East doth hold.
My love is such that rivers cannot quench,
Nor ought but love from thee, give recompense.

Thy love is such I can no way repay,
The heavens reward thee manifold, I pray.
Then while we live, in love let's so persevere
That when we live no more, we may live ever.

ANNE BRADSTREET

A Marriage Ring

The ring, so worn as you behold,
So thin, so pale, is yet of gold:
The passion such it was to prove —
Worn with life's care, love yet was love.

GEORGE CRABBE

Silver Wedding

The Silver Wedding! On some pensive ear
From towers remote as sound the silvery bells,
Today from one far unforgotten year
A silvery faint memorial music swells.
And silver-pale the slim memorial light
Of musing age on youthful joys is shed,
The golden joys of fancy's dawning bright,
The golden bliss of, Woo'd, and won, and wed.
Ah, golden hen, but silver now! In sooth,
The years that pale the cheek, that dim the eyes,
And silver o'er the golden hairs of youth,
Less prized can make its only priceless prize.

ARTHUR HUGH CLOUGH

Sympathy, sorrow and saying goodbye

Condolences

Offering your sympathy to someone who has lost a loved one can be a daunting task, but remember that all you need to do is show that you care. Cards and kind words can provide real comfort for those in mourning. Be sincere, and offer some practical help if you know them well and feel that is appropriate.

Don't say that you know what they're going through — everyone grieves in their own way — or offer clichés about feeling better in time. It may be true but it won't help them to hear it right now.

It can also help if you include something positive you remember about the deceased and how it made an impact on your life. The family may not know about the many ways in which the person touched others, and your memories can bring comfort at a difficult time. If in doubt, keep it short. A quote, religious verse or poem written in your own hand can make a card feel more personal than one that is just signed.

Spoken from the heart

I was so sorry to hear about your loss. It must be very sad for you and your family. You know I'm here for you if you ever need me.

◡

You and your family will be in our prayers.

◡

_____ touched our lives and will be greatly missed. I'll always remember his/her infectious laugh/generosity.

◡

I've been thinking of you since we heard the terrible news, and just wanted you to know that _____ will live on in our hearts.

◡

My sympathies for your loss.

◡

_____ was always thinking of others. I've never known anyone so kind, and we'll miss him greatly.

◡

I'm sure _____ would be touched to know how many friends are here today to say goodbye and show their support. Please call me if there's anything I can do in the next few weeks.

Written with care

We were so sad to hear about _____.
We just wanted to write and offer our deepest sympathy. He/she was a wonderful person who touched the lives of so many. If we can help you in some way over the next few weeks — even just by dropping round with a casserole — then please let us know. We are thinking of you and hope to see you soon.

Our sincere condolences to you and your family at this time. We hope that memories of the happy times you spent together will keep you close forever.

It is so difficult to lose someone you love. We are thinking of you in your time of sorrow and send all our love.

Our deepest sympathy to you (and your family).
We were so sorry to hear of the death
of _____. His/her sense of humour/love
of life/caring nature will be sorely missed
by so many.

⁓

I know that nothing I can say will take away
the pain of losing your beloved _____.
But I just wanted to let you know that you are
in my thoughts. Let me know when you're up to
a quiet visit. I would like to stop by with a warm
hug and shoulder to cry on, should you wish it.

⁓

Though we can't fully share the pain you
must be feeling, please let us offer you some
practical help in the days head. If you would
like some company, or some help getting the
house ready before the relatives arrive, please
don't hesitate to call.

⁓

I am so sorry for your loss. _____ will
live on in the lessons she taught her students/
work she did with old people/memories of
all her friends.

⁓

We remember _____ as a vibrant, loving person with a wonderful sense of humour/ generous nature. We hope that all the lovely memories you have of his/her life will help ease the pain of your loss.

⤳

_____ will never be forgotten.
With deepest sympathy, _____.

⤳

Please accept our heartfelt sympathies on your recent loss. We know how much you wanted this child, and how difficult it must be to have your dream snatched away. When you feel up to a quiet visit, please let us know. All our love.

⤳

We were shocked to hear the awful news about _____ and are heartbroken to think of you losing such a loveable, bright and charming son/daughter/cousin. There are no words that can express our sympathy for such a devastating loss, but please know that we are thinking of you at this terrible time. Our sincere condolences.

⤳

_____ was tireless in his/her devotion to others and will be sorely missed at the office/ club/school/pub. You are in our thoughts at this difficult time.

Quotable quotes

Death is not the last sleep.

It is the final awakening.

SIR WALTER SCOTT

⌒

Death is the veil which those who live call life:

They sleep, and it is lifted.

PERCY BYSSHE SHELLEY

⌒

Winter is on my head, but eternal spring is in my heart. The nearer I approach the end, the plainer I hear around me the immortal symphonies of the worlds which invite me.

VICTOR HUGO

⌒

Fear no more the heat o' the sun
Nor the furious winter's rages;
Thou thy worldly task hast done,
Home art gone and ta'en thy wages.

WILLIAM SHAKESPEARE

Be the green grass above me
With showers and dewdrops wet;
And if thou wilt, remember,
And if thou wilt, forget.

CHRISTINA ROSETTI

We sometimes congratulate ourselves at the
moment of waking from a troubled dream;
it may be so the moment after death.

NATHANIEL HAWTHORNE

In others' words

But a Short Time to Live

Our little hour, — how swift it flies
When poppies flare and lilies smile;
How soon the fleeting minute dies,
Leaving us but a little while
To dream our dream, to sing our song,
To pick the fruit, to pluck the flower,
The Gods — They do not give us long,—
One little hour.

Our little hour, — how short it is
When Love with dew-eyed loveliness
Raises her lips for ours to kiss
And dies within our first caress.
Youth flickers out like wind-blown flame,
Sweets of to-day to-morrow sour,
For Time and Death, relentless, claim
Our little hour.

Our little hour, — how short a time
To wage our wars, to fan our hates,
To take our fill of armoured crime,
To troop our banners, storm the gates.
Blood on the sword, our eyes blood-red,
Blind in our puny reign of power,

Do we forget how soon is sped
Our little hour?

Our little hour, — how soon it dies:
How short a time to tell our beads,
To chant our feeble Litanies,
To think sweet thoughts, to do good deeds.
The altar lights grow pale and dim,
The bells hang silent in the tower —
So passes with the dying hymn
Our little hour.

LESLIE COULSON

～

After life's fitful fever, he sleeps well;
Treason has done his worst: nor steel,
nor poison,
Malice domestic, foreign levy, nothing
Can touch him further.

Macbeth, WILLIAM SHAKESPEARE

～

I Did Not Die

Do not stand at my grave and forever weep.
I am not there; I do not sleep.
I am a thousand winds that blow.
I am the diamond glints on snow.
I am the sunlight on ripened grain.
I am the gentle autumn's rain.
When you awaken in the morning's hush
I am the swift uplifting rush
Of quiet birds in circled flight.
I am the soft stars that shine at night.
Do not stand at my grave and forever cry.
I am not there. I did not die.

MELINDA SUE PACHO

～

I lingered around them, under that benign
sky: watched the moths fluttering among the
hearth and harebells; listened to the soft wind
breathing through the grass; and wondered
how anyone could ever imagine unquiet
slumbers for the sleepers in that quiet earth.

Wuthering Heights, EMILY BRONTË

～

A Thought On Death

When life as opening buds is sweet,
And golden hopes the fancy greet,
And Youth prepares his joys to meet, —
Alas! how hard it is to die!

When just is seized some valued prize,
And duties press, and tender ties
Forbid the soul from earth to rise,—
How awful then it is to die!

When, one by one, those ties are torn,
And friend from friend is snatched forlorn,
And man is left alone to mourn, —
Ah then, how easy 'tis to die!

When faith is firm, and conscience clear,
And words of peace the spirit cheer,
And visioned glories half appear, —
'Tis joy, 'tis triumph then to die.

When trembling limbs refuse their weight,
And films, slow gathering, dim the sight,
And clouds obscure the mental light, —
'Tis nature's precious boon to die.

ANNA LAETITIA BARBAULD

⤳

Death is nothing at all. It does not count. I have only slipped away into the next room. Nothing has happened. Everything remains exactly as it was. I am I, and you are you, and the old life that we lived so fondly together is untouched, unchanged. Whatever we were to each other, that we are still. Call me by the old familiar name. Speak of me in the easy way which you always used. Put no difference into your tone. Wear no forced air of solemnity or sorrow. Laugh as we always laughed at the little jokes that we enjoyed together. Play, smile, think of me, pray for me. Let my name be ever the household word that it always was. Let it be spoken without an effort, without the ghost of a shadow upon it. Life means all that it ever meant. It is the same as it ever was. There is absolute and unbroken continuity. What is this death but a negligible accident? Why should I be out of mind because I am out of sight? I am but waiting for you, for an interval, somewhere very near, just around the corner. All is well. Nothing is hurt; nothing is lost. One brief moment and all will be as it was before. How we shall laugh at the trouble of parting when we meet again!

HENRY SCOTT HOLLAND

Sympathy

If someone has suffered a stroke of ill
fortune – perhaps the loss of their job,
divorce or illness – they will always
appreciate an expression of sympathy
and support. Be direct in what you say,
but be tactful. Don't dig for more
information than they may be willing
to share but let them know you're there
if they want to talk. And if you're writing,
rather than speaking to them personally,
make it clear that you don't expect a
reply – just that you're thinking of
them and that you care.

Spoken from the heart

I was so sorry to hear about you and _____.
I've known both of you for a long time and
I just wanted you to know that there is no
question of taking sides. You are both my
friends, and if there's anything I can do
to help, please let me know.

⌒

It must have been a great shock when the accident
happened/the redundancy was announced/the
diagnosis was made. If you ever need someone
to talk to, I'll always be here for you.

⌒

You must be very disappointed about the
restructuring at work, particularly after all the
long hours and effort you put in. You're great
at your job and you've had so much experience
that I'm confident you'll do
well wherever you are.

⌒

I heard about your bad luck with _____.
It's awful when something like that happens and
I really admire the way you are handling it.

⌒

I know we haven't seen you for ages, but we've
been thinking of you and how difficult it must
be looking after your sick son/aged mother.
It must be very tiring — is there anything
we can do to help?

⌒

Now must be an incredibly tough time for you.
Please make sure you're taking plenty of time
out to look after yourself. If we can help by
babysitting/driving to the hospital, or if you
simply want some company, please just ask.

⌒

Written with care

I'm so sorry to hear about _____.
I can imagine how difficult it must be and
I wish you all the best.

⌒

It's impossible to say anything of real comfort
at this time, but we just wanted to let you know
that we're thinking of you and hoping that life
takes an upward turn for you soon.

⌒

Thinking of you during this difficult time.
If anyone can get through this, it's you.

⌒

No matter how grim things get, I hope you
know that I'm always here for you.

⌒

I know they say that some things were sent
to test us. You've shown your true colours
throughout this trial and we think you
are a star!

⌒

You are handling your illness/misfortune
in a very courageous way. You are an
inspiration to us all. I hope things take a
turn for the better very soon.

⌒

I'm so sorry to hear that you're not well/having
a hard time — please ring me if you would like
some company, but I'll understand if you don't
feel like it at the moment. Just know that you're
not alone and that I'm hoping everything turns
out well for you.

⌒

I can't describe the pain and sadness I feel for you. The times ahead will be difficult but please know that you don't have to go through this alone. You are in my thoughts and I will be there to help you whenever you need me.

⌢

Some people will do anything to get breakfast in bed/a week off work. Get better soon!

Quotable quotes

A rooster one day; a feather duster the next; a phoenix the day after that.

ANON.

⌢

The journey is the reward.

CHINESE PROVERB

⌢

Love comforteth, like sunshine after rain.

Venus and Adonis, WILLIAM SHAKESPEARE

⌢

Earth hath no sorrow that heaven cannot heal.

SIR THOMAS MORE

❧

To everything there is a season, and a time
to every purpose under heaven.

The Bible, ECCLESIASTES 3:1

In others' words

We, ignorant of ourselves,
Beg often our own harms, which the
wise powers
Deny us for our own good; so we find we profit
By losing of our prayers.

WILLIAM SHAKESPEARE

❧

The beauty of the soul shines out when
a man bears with composure one heavy
mischance after another, not because he
does not feel them, but because he is a
man of high and heroic temper.

ARISTOTLE

❧

Oh benefit of ill! Now I find true
That better is by evil made better still.

WILLIAM SHAKESPEARE

⤴

More skilful in self-knowledge,
even more pure,
As tempted more; more able to endure,
As more exposed to suffering and distress;
Thence also, more alive to tenderness.

WILLIAM WORDSWORTH

⤴

Whether we be young or old,
Our destiny, our being's heart and home,
Is with infinitude, and only there;
With hope it is, hope that can never die,
Effort, and expectation, and desire,
And something evermore about to be.

WILLIAM WORDSWORTH

⤴

Tears, idle tears, I know not what they mean,
Tears from the depths of some divine despair
    Rise in the heart and gather to the eyes,
    In looking on the happy Autumn-fields,
And thinking of the days that are no more.

ALFRED TENNYSON

⌒

Reflect upon your present blessings, of
which every man has plenty; not on your past
misfortunes, of which all men have some.

CHARLES DICKENS

⌒

The greater the difficulty, the more glory
in surmounting it. Skilful pilots gain their
reputation from storms and tempests.

EPICTETUS

Goodbyes

How you say farewell to someone you love dearly is entirely different to a message scribbled in a goodbye card to a colleague at work. For someone you only know vaguely, stick to general best wishes for their future. Even if you don't like them all that much, keep it simple and sincere. You never know when or where you will meet them again.

Choosing the right words to end a relationship is a tough call. Be honest, be direct and be very clear that there will be no going back. It may seem kinder to fudge your feelings, but in the long run it's better to tell the truth. Never dump someone by email or phone, unless you have absolutely no other option; if you cared enough to be with them in the first place, you should care enough for their dignity and feelings to say it to their face.

Spoken from the heart

We won't forget you — but just in case,
write to us soon.

⌐

We'll miss your happy face around the place.

⌐

Wherever you end up, I know you'll make
a great impression.

⌐

I've enjoyed the time we've spent together but
I realise I still have feelings for my ex and I
don't think it's fair for me to keep seeing you.

⌐

I'm sorry, but my feelings aren't strong enough
to take our friendship to the next level. I think
it's best if we stop seeing each other.

⌐

Because I respect you and wouldn't ever cheat
on you, I want to tell you that I developed
feelings for someone else and can't keep
seeing you.

⌐

I've had a great time with you but I don't think we're right together in the long term. You deserve to be with someone who is absolutely right for you.

∽

The office/club/kindergarten won't be the same without you!

Written with care

As Lord Byron said 'All farewells should be sudden.' Bye.

∽

Best wishes on the next stage of your life journey. Travel safely and never forget the friends/colleagues you left behind.

∽

Even though you're leaving us, you'll always be here in our memories.

∽

Thanks so much for all you have done in your time here; it won't be forgotten.

∽

You brightened our days and lightened
our workload. You're going to be missed
around the office.

⌒

It has been such a pleasure working with you.
And even more fun socialising.

⌒

Happy retirement and here's to a job well done.

⌒

Have a wonderful trip and although I can't
be with you, my thoughts will be.

⌒

All the best on your travels and remember that
even if things don't go to plan, you'll have lots
of great stories to tell on your return.

⌒

Saying goodbye is hard, especially when we
don't know when we'll see each other again.
But whether it's a week, a month, or a year,
I know our friendship/love/relationship will
be unchanged. Bon voyage.

⌒

Saying 'Goodbye' sounds so final; so let's
just say 'Fare Well' instead.

Quotable quotes

Parting is to die a little.

FRENCH PROVERB

⌁

Love knows not its own depth until
the hour of separation.
All farewells should be sudden.

LORD BYRON

⌁

I do desire we may be better strangers.

As You Like It, WILLIAM SHAKESPEARE

⌁

Laughter is not at all a bad beginning
for a friendship, and it is far the best
ending for one.

OSCAR WILDE

In others' words

Why should a foolish marriage vow
Which long ago was made,
Oblige us to each other now
When passion is decayed?
We loved, and we loved, as long as we could,
Till our love was loved out in us both,
But our marriage is dead,
when the pleasure is fled:
'Twas pleasure first made it an oath.

A Foolish Marriage Vow, JOHN DRYDEN

~

When love grows diseas'd, the best thing
we can do is put it to a violent death;
I cannot endure the torture of a lingering
and consumptive passion.

SIR GEORGE ETHEREGE

Thanks, praise and apologies

Congratulations

A friend gets a new job, your boss
receives an award, a family member wins
Tattslotto — now's the time you need to
step in with some heartfelt words of
praise to mark the occasion. Long after
the cheque has been spent or the cup
has become tarnished with age, they'll
remember the fact that you cared enough
to share in their triumph.

A brief note or phone call is fine or, if you
don't know the person particularly well,
perhaps a short email. Do it promptly
though, and make sure to say how
delighted you are with their good and
well-deserved fortune.

Spoken from the heart

If anyone deserves this award/promotion/prize, it's you. You've worked hard and should relish every moment of it.

~

Enjoy your moment in the sun. I saw how hard you worked for it and you've definitely earned it.

~

Congratulations! It's so good to hear about your promotion/new house/award.

~

I knew there was a reason why I stuck with you through all the tough times! Congratulations on a job well done!

~

I just wanted you to know how proud and happy I was to hear that you've been promoted/won an award.

~

Well done! It was a fantastic performance/speech/achievement/result!

~

Congratulations! We're almost as proud
as you must be!

⌢

Hooray for you! Others would have given
it up as all too hard, so well done for going
after your dreams. Enjoy your achievement.

Written with care

Be proud of all that you've accomplished.
We certainly are.

⌢

To the girl/guy most likely to succeed —
you've done it!

⌢

Congratulations on your promotion.
You're the perfect person for the job.

⌢

Well done on making it to the place you
always wanted to be. May it be everything
you dreamed of — and much more.

⌢

Best wishes for a great future. Wherever
the road leads from here, we know you'll
take the right turning every time.

～

Wishing you happiness and great joy as you
celebrate a tremendous achievement.

～

We're thinking of you on this great day and are
there with you in spirit. Have one for us!

～

My most sincere congratulations. All of your
hard work and patience has finally paid off and
I'm very proud of you. May this be the first
of many more successes in the future.

～

What you have achieved has highlighted the
importance of following your dreams and
doing what you love. You're an inspiration!

～

I was so happy to hear about your news.
Let's celebrate!

～

Congratulations on receiving the award. That's
terrific news. I was so happy for you when
I saw the announcement in the paper. Hope
everything else in your life is going just as well.

Quotable quotes

There is always room at the top.

DANIEL WEBSTER

⤳

We are what we repeatedly do. Excellence,
then, is not an act, but a habit.

ARISTOTLE

⤳

The happiest people in life don't have the
best of everything . . . they make the best
of everything they have. Congratulations
on doing the best of all!

ANON.

⤳

Well done is better than well said.

BENJAMIN FRANKLIN

⤳

Great men are meteors designed to burn
so that the earth may be lighted.

NAPOLEON BONAPARTE

In others' words

Success: To laugh often and much, to win the
respect of intelligent people and the affection
of children, to earn the appreciation of honest
critics and endure the betrayal of false friends,
to appreciate beauty, to find the best in others,
to leave the world a bit better, whether by a
healthy child, a garden patch, or a redeemed
social condition; to known even one life has
breathed easier because you have lived.
This is to have succeeded!

RALPH WALDO EMERSON

If a man write a better book, preach a better
sermon, or make a better mouse-trap than
his neighbour, tho' he build his house in
the woods, the world will make a beaten path
to his door.

RALPH WALDO EMERSON

To burn always with this hard gem-like flame,
to maintain this ecstasy, is success in life.

WALTER HORATIO PATER

❧

Knowledge dwells
In heads replete with thoughts of other men;
Wisdom in minds attentive to their own.

WILLIAM COWPER

❧

To travel hopefully is a better thing than
to arrive, and the true success is to labour.

ROBERT LOUIS STEVENSON

❧

Life affords no higher pleasure than that
of surmounting difficulties, passing from
one step of success to another, forming new
wishes and seeing them gratified.

SAMUEL JOHNSON

❧

'Tis not in mortals to command success,
But we'll do more Sempronius; we'll deserve it.

JOSEPH ADDISON

❧

A victory is twice itself when the achiever
brings home full numbers.

WILLIAM SHAKESPEARE

෴

I held it truth, with him who sings
To one clear harp in divers tones,
That men may rise on stepping-stones
Of their dead selves to higher things.

ALFRED TENNYSON

෴

The most successful men in the end are those
whose success is the result of steady accretion.
It is the man who carefully advances step by
step, with his mind becoming wider and
wider — and progressively better able to grasp
any theme or situation — persevering in what
he knows to be practical, and concentrating his
thought upon it, who is bound to succeed in
the greatest degree.

ALEXANDER GRAHAM BELL

Thanks

If you've received a compliment, a present or a favour, then a few words of thanks are definitely in order. How formal your response should be depends on the situation. For a stay with friends, a brief handwritten note would be appropriate. For a favour done by a colleague, a chatty email might suffice. For a really thoughtful present or huge favour, write a longer note on classy stationery, and bestow with a gift or bunch of flowers. They'll be pleasantly surprised and will remember your politeness.

Spoken from the heart

Thanks so much for all your help. I couldn't have done it without you and I really appreciate the time you put in.

⌒

I hope you know how much your help/ contribution/kindness has meant to me. You deserve a big round of applause too.

⌒

You've been so kind, I can hardly think of how to thank you enough. So I'll just say 'thank you' and leave the rest to your imagination!

⌒

How did you know we needed _____? We'll cherish your thoughtfulness always.

⌒

I'll treasure the book/painting/paperweight you gave me. It will always remind me of you.

⌒

The reference you gave me must have been brilliant — I got offered the job yesterday, so thanks!

⌒

You shouldn't have done it, but since you did, can I just say that your choice was absolutely inspired!

⁓

We will never forget the gorgeous scenery and the fabulous meal you whipped up on Saturday night — thanks so much for inviting us to your beach house last weekend.

Written with care

What a delicious and memorable dinner you prepared for us! The beef/cacciatore/lasagne was fantastic. Hope the cleaning up didn't take you too long! See you soon.

⁓

So what is your secret recipe for holding such fantastic parties? The food was first rate, the guests were fascinating and you looked incredibly calm, cool and collected throughout it all. I just hope the red wine comes out of the carpet! Thanks again for a great night.

⁓

Thanks for such a wonderful few days. I'd
happily do it all again next weekend but you put
so much effort into making sure we had a good
time that you really deserve to put your feet up!

⌇

Thank you for all your help with fixing
my computer/painting my apartment. I am
now able to work on that project/redecorate
the rooms. I'll never forget your kindness
in sharing your time and energy.

⌇

Thank you so much for the wonderful vase/
watch/ornament. Every time I look at it,
I'll think of you and your kindness.

⌇

Many thanks for your caring actions and loving
words. I appreciate having such a good friend.

⌇

Just when I needed you most, you were there.
Thank you.

⌇

I just wanted to thank you so much for the
_____. We've wanted one of those for ages.
It was so incredibly thoughtful of you. Someday
soon you must come around and see it in pride
of place. Thanks again.

⌒

The kindness and generosity you showed to
all of us when _____ died was much
appreciated. The plant was a wonderful
idea — I've planted it in the garden and
every time it flowers, I'll think of him and
of you. Thanks too for the casserole, your
heartfelt letter and for your support.
You're a true friend.

⌒

Thanks for the wonderful present you sent
_____. I know she will treasure it all her
life. We're all settled in happily at home now
and would love you to come by and say hello
to the newest family member. Call me soon.

Quotable quotes

The hands that help are holier than
the lips that pray.

ROBERT G. INGERSOLL

⌁

After a good dinner, one can forgive anybody,
even one's own relations.

OSCAR WILDE

⌁

A man hath no better thing under the sun
than to eat and to drink and to be merry.

The Bible, ECCLESIASTES 8:15

⌁

Fish and visitors smell in three days.

BENJAMIN FRANKLIN

In others' words

For this relief much thanks; 'tis bitter cold,
And I am sick at heart.

WILLIAM SHAKESPEARE

⌒

Our deeds still travel with us from afar,
And what we have been makes us what we are.

GEORGE ELIOT

⌒

What more felicity can fall to creature,
Than to enjoy delight with liberty.

EDMUND SPENSER

⌒

That best portion of a good man's life,
His little, nameless, unremembered acts
Of kindness and of love.

WILLIAM WORDSWORTH

⌒

One man gives freely, yet grows all the richer;
another withholds what he should give,
and only suffers want.

The Bible, PROVERBS: 11:24

⌒

A good deed is never lost. He who sows courtesy, reaps friendship; he who plants kindness, gathers love; pleasure bestowed on a grateful mind was never sterile, but generally gratitude begets reward.

SAINT BASIL

Apologies

'I'm sorry', is perhaps the hardest thing to say. In most cases it's best said in person so that the person can see that you are genuinely remorseful for your error or any pain you may have caused. If you write something, keep it short and never make excuses. Remember, the point is to earn forgiveness, not score points — when offered a heartfelt apology, most people will be willing to forgive if not forget. And even if they don't, at least you will know that you've done the right thing and tried your best.

Spoken from the heart

I am so sorry for hurting you. It was thoughtless
and insensitive of me not to consider
your feelings.

⌇

I know that saying sorry can't repair the
damage I caused, but please know that I will do
everything I can to make things right again.

⌇

I hope you can forgive what I said and that our
friendship/working relationship/relationship
won't be affected.

⌇

I was completely out of line last night.
I hope my remarks didn't cause you too much
offence and that you managed to have a great
night anyway.

⌇

I don't like being in your bad
books — particularly because it was all my fault.
Can I make it up to you by inviting you over
for dinner/replacing the figurine?

⌇

I didn't mention it last night as I didn't want
to spoil the fun you were having, but I
accidentally broke one of your glasses/spilt
red wine on your carpet/knocked over the pot
plant. I'm sorry for my clumsiness and I'd like
to offer to replace it for you/have the damage
repaired. Again, my apologies, and please
let me know where I can find a replacement/
organise repairs.

❧

I am a blithering idiot and my only saving
grace is that I recognise the fact. Will you
please forgive me?

❧

I'm hurting because I hurt you. I'm sorry
and I hope you can forgive me.

❧

I don't blame you for being upset. I only
realised later how my remarks must have
sounded, and I'm really sorry.

Written with care

I am sorry for what I did the other day/night/
week. I'll understand if you don't want to talk
to me right now, but please feel that you always
can. I would never want to jeopardise our
friendship/love, which is why I wanted to let
you know how deeply sorry I am.

⌒

I know they say that 'sorry' is the hardest word
to say, but please believe me when I say that
I am truly sorry for what I did.

⌒

If I could take back what I said/did, I would.
Please forgive me.

⌒

There is no excuse for how I behaved.
Please accept my sincere apology.

⌒

Although I apologised to you last night for the
loud music from our house-warming party,
I want you to know how sorry we are and to
assure you that it won't happen again.

⌒

I apologise from the bottom of my heart
(which is currently in my boots). Please,
I beg you, give me another chance.

⌒

You know I would never do anything to
deliberately hurt you. I can only say that
I was careless and inconsiderate and faithfully
promise to never to be angry with you again/do
the dishes every night for a month.

⌒

I feel dreadful about ruining our night out
by arguing with _____ about _____.
You were absolutely right to point out that
it was none of my business, and I apologise
sincerely for ignoring old friendship and good
manners in talking that way. The start of the
evening was wonderful, and I loved catching
up with so many familiar faces. I hope you can
forgive me for spoiling the last part of the night
through my thoughtlessness.

⌒

I apologise for not turning up at dinner the other night. There is no excuse for not ringing to let you know. All I can say is that _____ was ill with _____ and between driving to the doctor and soothing his/her fevered brow, I completely forgot that we had made an arrangement. Can we reschedule for this week instead? Thanks – and again, I am so sorry.

Quotable quotes

Forgiveness is the fragrance the violet sheds on the heel that has crushed it.

MARK TWAIN

⌇

Always forgive your enemies; nothing annoys them so much.

OSCAR WILDE

⌇

'I can forgive, but I cannot forget', is only another way of saying, 'I cannot forgive.'

ELBERT HUBBARD

⌇

How shall I lose the sin, yet keep the sense,
And love the offender, yet detest the offence?

ALEXANDER POPE

⌒

Universal reproach (far worse to
bear than violence).

JOHN MILTON

In others' words

The web of our life is of a mingled yarn,
good and ill together: our virtues would
be proud if our faults whipped them not;
and our crimes would despair if they were
not cherished by our own virtues.

WILLIAM SHAKESPEARE

⌒

This is certain, that a man that studieth
revenge keeps his wounds green, which
otherwise would heal and do well.

FRANCIS BACON

⌒

Good, to forgive;
Best, to forget!
Living, we fret;
Dying, we live!

ROBERT BROWNING

～

To me
His all fault who hath no fault at all:
For who loves me must have a touch of earth.

ALFRED TENNYSON

～

And throughout all Eternity
I forgive you, you forgive me.
As our dear Redeemer said:
'This is the Wine, and this is the Bread.'

I will not willing offend,
Nor be easily offended;
What's amiss I'll strive to mend,
And endure what can't be mended.

ISAAC WATTS

～

Vice is a monster of so frightful mien,
As to be hated needs but to be seen;
Yet seen too oft, familiar with her face,
We first endure, then pity, then embrace.

ALEXANDER POPE

⌇

Wilt thou forgive that sin, where I begun,
Which is my sin, though it were done before?
Wilt thou forgive those sins through which
I run?
And do them still, though still I do deplore?
When thou hast done, thou hast not done,
For I have more.

JOHN DONNE

Invitations and replies

Knowing how to word an invitation is not always easy, and it's important that you include all the necessary details.

Knowing how to reply to an invitation is a sure sign of good manners. The first rule is, you *must* respond, even if you can't or don't want to attend the event. Secondly, you should respond in kind — if you're sent a formal invite, send a formal written reply that mimics the form of the one sent to you. If it's a two-line email from a friend inviting you round for a barbie, feel free to give a quick call or to shoot an email back.

Always take note of any RSVP date and if you think you are going to be late to the event, be sure to spell out what time you think you'll arrive — you don't want to inconvenience your hosts or any other guests. Likewise, if you need to cancel at the last minute, give as much notice as you can and only do so for a decent reason such as sickness, not just a better offer. (Unless it's a really good friend who'll be excited that you're going on a hot date instead!)

Spoken from the heart

What a great idea! I'd love to come. Is there anything I can bring or do to help you prepare for the occasion?

⌒

The party/house-warming sounds wonderful. I need to look at my diary though, so can I get back to you by Wednesday with a definite answer?

⌒

What a shame! We'd love to be able to come but unfortunately we have something else on that night.

⌒

Thanks for asking me out, but I actually have a husband/wife/boyfriend/girlfriend. I'm flattered by the invitation though.

⌒

Thanks for your offer but I'd prefer that we just remain friends.

⌒

Thanks, but unfortunately I have other plans.

Written with care

Please join us for dinner on _____
at ___ am/pm. We're celebrating _____
and would be delighted if you could join us.

⤳

I will be delighted to have dinner with you on
_____. Thanks so much for thinking of
me. I'm looking forward to catching up on all
your news and celebrating _____ with you.

⤳

_____ and I accept with pleasure your
kind invitation to a celebration of _____
on _____ at ___ am/pm.

⤳

I'm looking forward to your engagement party.
Thanks for including me in this
special occasion.

⤳

Thanks so much for thinking of me but sadly I
won't be able to make it. I'll write more when
things have calmed down at work/I've recovered
from my illness/I'm back from holiday.

⤳

We accept your kind invitation with
great pleasure.

⌐

I appreciate very much — and accept — your
kind invitation to _____.

⌐

Thank you for inviting me to present the
results of my research/speak about my
experiences overseas. I am happy to accept
and will discuss, as you suggested, _____.
I'm not sure how much time you have allocated
for this — please let me know.

Invitations

Birthday

Share the fun of Peter's 5th birthday!
Sunday, November 28th
4 p.m.
16 Bayview Road
Seaford

RSVP 5555 1234 by 14th November

⌐

Please join us in celebrating Peter's 10th birthday
Sunday, November 28th
4–6 p.m.
Claire's house
16 Bayview Road
Seaford

⌒

Please join us for a birthday dinner
In honour of
Claire's 50th
Sunday, November 28th at 7 p.m.
16 Bayview Road
Seaford

RSVP 5555 1234

⌒

In case you didn't know
Peter is about to hit the big 4-0!
Help us celebrate with a surprise party
On Sunday, November 28th, 2007 at 8 p.m.
16 Bayview Road
Seaford

RSVP 5555 1234 by 14th November

Shhh! He doesn't know!

Rite of passage

You are invited to join us
As our son Peter is baptised
On Sunday, November 28th
11 a.m.
Church
16 Bayview Road
Seaford
John and Catherine Smith

RSVP 5555 1234

⌐

With great pleasure and pride
We invite you to share a special moment
in our lives
When our son Peter
Is called to the Torah as a Bar Mitzvah
On Sunday 28th November 2007
16 Bayview Road, Seaford
John and Catherine Smith

Engagement

Please join us for an engagement party
Honouring Peter and Claire
On November 28th, 2007
At 8 p.m.
16 Bayview Road
Seaford

⁓

Please join us in celebrating our engagement
At 16 Bayview Road
Seaford
On November 28th, 2007
Peter Smith and Claire Roberts
RSVP 5555 1234

Wedding

Mr and Mrs Roberts
request the honour of your presence
at the marriage of their daughter
Claire
to
Peter
Son of Mr and Mrs Smith
At Church
16 Bayview Road, Seaford
On Sunday November 28th, 2007

RSVP 5555 1234

⌒

John and Catherine Smith, together with
David and Janet Roberts
Would be honoured to have you share
in the joy of the marriage of their children,
Peter and Claire
On Sunday 28th November, 2007
At Church
16 Bayview Road, Seaford

RSVP 5555 1234

⌒

Peter and Claire
Invite you
To witness their wedding
And celebrate the beginning of their
new life together
At 3.30 p.m. on Sunday 28th November, 2007
Gardens
Bayview Road, Seaford
RSVP 5555 1234

Golden Wedding Anniversary

The Smith family invites you to help celebrate
Catherine and John's Golden Wedding
Anniversary.
An open house will be held at
16 Bayview Road, Seaford
from 1–4pm on Sunday 28th November, 2007.
Children welcome.

Responses to invitations

Peter Smith
Accepts with pleasure
David and Janet Roberts'
Kind invitation to dinner
On the 28th of November at 8 p.m.
But regrets that
Claire
Will be unable to attend.

~

Peter Smith
Regrets that he is unable to accept
The kind invitation of
Mr and Mrs David Roberts
To the marriage of their daughter
Claire
Sunday the 28th of November, 2007

~

David and Janet Roberts
Accept with pleasure
The kind invitation of
Peter Smith and Julia Thomas
To their marriage on
Sunday, 28th November, 2007
At 8 p.m.
Church
16 Bayview Road
Seaford

Religious celebrations and cultural festivals

Celebrations

Special occasions such as Christmas,
Diwali and Hannukah are often marked
by the exchange of cards and greetings.
The following section includes seasonal
greetings, plus suggestions for what to say
to mark different religious festivals and
rites of passage.

Christmas and New Year

Christmas is a christian holiday celebrating the birth of Christ. The New Year celebrates the end of one year and the beginning of the next.

May Christmas bring you everything your heart desires.

⁓

Wishing you a Christmas filled with good cheer and great food!

⁓

Happy Christmas! May your stocking be stuffed with love, happiness and fun.

⁓

May the end of the year draw to a happy close, and the new one start with joy.

⁓

Here's hoping your stocking is full of presents
and your home filled with love and laughter
this Christmas

⌒

May the coming year be filled with prosperity,
joy and friends.

⌒

Joy to the world – and lots and lots to
you and your family too.

⌒

Wishing you a Merry Christmas, and thank you
for your friendship throughout the year.

⌒

From our hearts to yours, we send love and
best wishes for Christmas and the New Year.

Passover

An eight-day Jewish festival celebrating
the deliverance of the Israelites from
slavery in Egypt.

At this season of promise, may your love
be rekindled, your hopes be renewed and
your strength refreshed.

～

Wishing you peace, strength and blessings
in abundance this Passover — and always!

～

We are thinking of you at this special time, as
always. Best wishes for this beautiful season.

～

May Passover bring you and your family
contentment, joy and peace.

～

Wishing you a holiday filled with
love and laughter.

Hanukkah

Hanukkah, or the festival of lights, is an
eight-day Jewish holiday that celebrates
religious freedom and the end of Greek rule
over a holy temple in Jerusalem in 165 BC.

Best wishes for a happy Hanukkah to
you and your family.

Ᏽ

May the candle shine brightly for
you on Hanukkah.

Ᏽ

Wishing you and your family peace
and happiness on Hanukkah.

Ᏽ

Just as the Hanukkah candle shines, so too does
your love/friendship/support light up my life.

Ᏽ

Here's to eight days and nights of happiness
at Hanukkah!

Diwali

Diwali is the five-day Hindu festival of lights, which celebrates the victory of good over evil — particularly the homecoming of the divine King Rama and his queen Sita after fourteen years of exile. It is also an important festival in the Sikh religion.

May your face shine brightly throughout the festival of light and the coming year.

⌒

Best wishes for Diwali. May it be the beginning of a year filled with happiness and prosperity.

⌒

Warmest wishes to you and your family at Diwali. May you all be showered with presents, happiness and smiles.

⌒

May the festival of light bring happiness, riches and love to you and your family.

Eid Al-Fitr

Eid Al-Fitr, or the Celebration of Breaking the
Fast, marks the end of the Muslim religious
event of Ramadan, the month of fasting.

May Eid bring you together with all those
you love, to celebrate this happy day.

⁓

Wishing you a joyful Eid and happiness
throughout the year.

⁓

Best wishes to you and your family
on this joyful and blessed day.

⁓

May success and joy be your companions
on this holy day of celebration.

Chinese New Year

Chinese New Year celebrations are a family affair, which honour Heaven and Earth, the gods of the household and the family ancestors. Festivities begin with the New Moon on the first day of the Chinese calendar's New Year and end fifteen days later with a Lantern Festival.

May this next year be filled with prosperity, joy and fun.

～

Have a wonderful Year of the _____ and may it be your best one yet.

～

Sending you best wishes for health, wealth and happiness in the new year.

～

Wishing you a year that is filled with everything you wish for yourself.

～

Here's to a New Year filled with blessings and happiness.

Christening

Christening is a ceremony where a child or adult is baptised and given a Christian name as a sign of their membership of the Christian church.

Congratulations and best wishes on your baby's christening.

～

Let's wet the head of the newest member of your family. Thank you so much for including us in this special occasion.

～

Wishing all the very best in life to little _____ on the occasion of her/his christening.

～

May little _____ have a blessed life, full of love, laughter, family and friends.

～

Here's to a life of faith, hope and happiness for Baby _____.

Bar/Bat Mitzvah

A Bar Mitzvah is a Jewish ceremony and celebration to mark the thirteenth birthday of a boy, who then assumes his full religious obligations. In some communities, Jewish girls celebrate a similar milestone at the age of twelve with a Bat Mitzvah.

Mazel Tov to you on your Bar Mitzvah!

❧

Congratulations on your Bar Mitzvah. We hope the knowledge that you've gained brings you success and happiness.

❧

As you celebrate your Bar Mitzvah, we're thinking of you with pride and love.

❧

Congratulations and may the Torah be your teacher as you go through life.

Confirmation and First Communion

A rite in some Christian churches, where a
baptised person is confirmed in their faith and
admitted to full membership of the church.

All our love on this special day. May you
be filled with faith and hope always.

～

Congratulations on your confirmation/first
communion. Best wishes for the future.

～

Welcome to the family of Christ!

～

Best wishes to you as you make a new beginning.
May God always watch over
you in the years to come.

Social
slips and
sticky topics

Awkward conversations

We all have to talk to people who are difficult or who we don't like very much — whether it be the girl who tormented you all through school, a lewd colleague, a cranky aunt or some other person with whom you have nothing in common. So how do you fill in those awkward silences? It may be a cliché, but the weather is not a bad start. It's neutral, you've both experienced it, and it might get the ball rolling.

Other topics that are good conversation starters include mutual friends or family, holidays, and work or study. If in doubt, ask them a personal question about something close to their heart (but not too personal!). Stay clear of sensitive issues such as politics (including office politics), contentious issues in the news, or why exactly you hate them so much. You don't want to start a brawl.

Remember, asking a question will put you in control of the direction the conversation takes (as well as taking the heat off you). Listen politely to the response, nod at appropriate moments and make your excuses to depart after a reasonable amount of time. You don't have to pretend to be best buddies, nor should you bolt for the door at the earliest opportunity. Just exchange a few brief comments, then move out of range with your grace and dignity intact.

I haven't seen you for ages. Have you heard
anything recently about a mutual friend/
colleague/old school teacher?

⌒

You look very relaxed/tanned. Have you
been away on holiday?

⌒

What a lovely tie/dress/haircut! Where did
you get it/done?

⌒

Are you still working at the same place?
Are you enjoying the job?

⌒

How are your kids doing? How old
are they now?

Unpleasant truths

Put simply, there is no easy way to tell someone they have bad breath, body odour or spinach stuck between their teeth. If you don't know the person that well, or it's inappropriate to mention it (like with your boss) try opening the windows or offering them some fresh-mint chewing gum and hope they get the hint.

For people you know well or work closely with, directness is probably the best way to get a result — but don't make a big deal out of it and definitely *don't* bring up the topic in front of others. You can even pretend you share the problem so they don't think that they are the only one.

Hey, do you want a free deodorant? I've just swapped to a new brand and they gave me a free one — it's fantastic. Before I used to get a bit pongy by the end of the day, but now there's no problem. Why don't you try it too?

~

As we're friends, I thought you'd rather hear it from me that sometimes your breath is a bit whiffy . . . I've had the same problem too, but my dentist/new brand of mouthwash/fresh breath mints seem to do the trick.

~

You probably need to know that there is a bit of spinach stuck between your teeth/lipstick on your collar/loo paper stuck to your heel.

'Foot-in-mouth' moments

As the old saying goes, when you find yourself in a hole, the best thing you can do is stop digging. So if you make an unintentional blunder, or insult someone without meaning to, don't go into lengthy explanations about what you said, or why you were inspired to say it. That will only make matters worse. Neither should you ignore your slip completely in the hopes they didn't notice. Believe me, they did.

The gracious thing to do after you've put your foot in your mouth is to apologise sincerely, ask forgiveness and hope that everyone can move on swiftly.

I am so sorry. I realise how bad that sounded and I certainly didn't mean to offend you.

⤳

That was extremely tactless of me, and I'm so sorry.

⤳

I was trying to be funny and got carried away. I didn't mean to hurt your feelings by suggesting anything offensive. You know that you are a dear friend/colleague and I'd never do anything to hurt you intentionally.

⤳

I'm sorry, my mind has gone blank. I know we've met before/known each other for twenty years but I have completely forgotten your name.

⤳

I didn't mean to criticise your girlfriend. Overall, I think she's fabulous.

⤳

Thanks for pointing out where I went wrong. Next time, I'll make sure I know all the facts before giving my opinion.

The morning after

Everyone makes mistakes — particularly
when alcohol is involved — but it's how
you handle them that shows what kind of
a person you really are. So whether you
threw a tantrum in front of your in-laws,
had one too many glasses of wine at the
office Christmas do, or did something
truly scary — like send a loving, late-night
text to an ex — the best thing to do is admit
your bad behaviour, offer to make amends
and promise not to do it again.

If you made a complete idiot of yourself,
or caused serious damage, think about
sending a card and perhaps a small gift
or flowers as well.

I behaved appalling last night and I apologise
for embarrassing you and your guests/family/
colleagues. Next time, I'll stay away from the
after-dinner drinks/tequila shooters.

⁓

I have a horrible feeling that I insulted you last
night. Please believe that it was only the drink
talking and I hope I didn't ruin the whole night
for you.

⁓

I hope you can forgive and forget my behaviour
last night. Perhaps it's a good thing I can't
remember it too well myself but I would
hate for my stupid behaviour to ruin a great
friendship/working relationship.

Unwanted advances

Assertiveness is the key here. If you don't
speak up, then you're only encouraging the
person to continue with the unwelcome
behaviour. The first step is to ask them
politely to stop and make it clear that
their actions are unwelcome. There is
legislation to protect against sexual
harassment in the workplace so talk
to someone in your Human Resources
department if there is a problem, and keep
a log of any incidents.

If you pat me on the bottom again/crack one more joke about my bra size, I'll shriek so loudly that it will be heard all the way to the HR department.

⌁

That kind of comment/behaviour is inappropriate. We are working colleagues and I would appreciate it if you kept our relationship strictly professional.

⌁

If you don't take your hand away this instant, you'll be wearing that drink on your head and your girlfriend will want to know the reason why.

⌁

Excuse me, but I'm really not interested. I have a boyfriend/girlfriend/husband/wife.

A friend in need

Sometimes you can see a friend is struggling — perhaps with an addiction, an eating disorder or a psychological problem. Ignoring the problem won't make it go away but you worry that if you say something, you may lose your friend all together. But friendship has its dues as well as its pleasures. Talk to a professional specialising in your friend's problem and get advice on how to approach the topic. It's important to show your friend that you care and are willing to talk about the problem. Do it in private and pick your moment carefully. Don't force your friend to talk to you if they are unwilling, but try to open up the lines of communication.

I can see that you're not very happy at the moment and I'm worried about you because you are my friend.

⌒

As a friend/sister/colleague, I hope you feel that you can confide in me. I'll understand if you choose not to talk to me about this, but have you considered talking to someone independently about anorexia/alcoholism?

⌒

I've noticed that your behaviour has changed over the last few months. I'm concerned that you're not well and would be happy to help you find someone to talk to about anger management/gambling addictions.

Personal questions

Just because someone asks you a personal question doesn't mean you have to answer it. So if you're asked a question about your sex life (or lack of it), personal finances or political beliefs, feel free to deflect the query with humour, politeness or a little blunt honesty.

I know a lot of people don't mind discussing how much they earn/how many times a week they have sex/what party they voted for last election, but I'm a little bit old-fashioned that way and I'd rather not.

~

If I told you the answer to that question, I'd have to kill you.

~

Even my husband/mother/hairdresser doesn't know how old I am/the answer to that.

~

I'm still single because I figure it's much better for my sex life.

Constructive criticism

No-one likes being criticised, but
if you deliver your observations in the
right way, you're far more likely to get
results. Start by saying something pleasant
about the person, then describe what
the problem is and why it's annoying you,
then finish up by expressing appreciation
for their efforts to change.

I think you're doing really well on cutting back on your smoking. Cigarette smoke gives me a headache so it would be great if you could smoke outside instead. I really appreciate that you're trying to quit and I'm sure we'll be able to work this out.

❧

That last project we did together went really well. I've been working around the clock on the new deal. If we went through the schedule and worked out how to divide the workload up, things might run more smoothly. Thanks for helping me work this out. I'm sure this will save us both a lot of time and effort.

❧

I love that new CD of yours. It does make it hard for me to study/concentrate/hear myself think though, so if you could put the headphones on, I'd really appreciate it. You have great taste in music and you can play it as loud as you like when I've finished here.

Escaping a bore

If you've been trapped in a corner by the office or party bore, then you need to regain control so that you can make your escape. Stop nodding your head or giving them any sort of encouragement to keep talking, wait for a break in their flow, then get ready to make your move. Start by saying something positive about the person or the conversation you were having, give a definite excuse for leaving, add one more positive comment and go.

It was great hearing all about your renovation.
I need to say hello to another couple of people
here. It was a pleasure seeing you again. Bye.

⌒

Excuse me, I can see someone over there
trying to get my attention.

⌒

How lovely to chat, but I'm afraid I need
to find the bathroom. It was a pleasure
talking to you.

⌒

May I get you a drink from the bar/cup of tea
from the buffet/plate of food?
*(Get an extra item while you're fulfilling your promise, then
say that you need to deliver the other one to someone else.
You'll come across as politeness personified and they can't
detain you without looking mean.)*